Old Fashioned Motherhood

Old Fashioned Motherhood

Baby and Child Care Advice from a New England Housewife

By Mrs. Sharon White

The Legacy of Home Press
puritanlight@gmail.com

The Legacy of Home Press
ISBN-13: 978-0692274736
ISBN-10: 0692274731
Old Fashioned Motherhood: Baby and Child Care Advice from a New England Housewife

Author – Mrs. Sharon White

[Cover photo: Library of Congress – 1942 baby in playpen]

Contents

I

Setting up a Home

There is nothing quite so exciting as setting up a home for baby's arrival. We anticipate many children to walk the halls and brighten our lives. Setting up rooms and creating an inviting, happy place- to- be is a wonderful way to strengthen family bonds, and make a house a real old fashioned home.

A humble baby's room would contain a crib, dressing table, and a rocking chair. If there is little money available, pretty old pictures from calendars could be put on the walls to decorate. "Precious Moments" is a favorite of mine. Have you heard of the "Hummel" figures of small children? I used to have an old clock with a "Hummel" painting of a sweet child in a raincoat and hat. It brought a warm smile to all who looked to see the time.

The dressing table had a nice thin mattress on the top. Often, there were shelves underneath. Here we had assorted old baskets full of undershirts, diapers, powder, baby lotion, baby oil, cotton balls, and all the things one would need to care for a sweet infant.

A nice rocking chair is a necessity. Rocking a baby for comfort, or to sleep, is a very important job for Mother. Here we would sing lullabies, and hold the infant, as if we had all the time in the world. I have 2 antique rocking chairs which came from my grandmothers. Of course, I don't let anyone but a mother sit on those delicate seats. They would break them for sure! (gentle smiles) I also have a newer, sturdier chair from almost 2 decades ago, which I bought at a garage sale. I picked up a nice painted white chair several years ago, for rocking on the porch. I gave this to one of my girls when she had her first baby.

It is so sweet to have a hand crocheted afghan to place over the side of a rocking chair. How many mothers have worked with pretty yarn, praying as they crocheted a baby blanket, while they waited for baby to be born? It is a wonderful tradition, and helps center the heart towards home.

If one cannot crochet, or is not inclined to do such work, a pretty chenille blanket would be just as lovely; just something to snuggle up with baby, or to keep warm while rocking, makes home sweeter.

Stores used to sell a variety of rocking chair seat cushions. These had little ties all around to attach to the different parts of the chair, and hold it in place. The cushions made the chairs very comfortable. Today's cushions are so plain looking, as it seems rocking chairs, and their accessories, are almost out of fashion. If you can find a pretty set of cushions for your chair, you would enjoy it so much more.

One sweet thing in a home for children is a small lamp with a dim light. A 40- watt bulb would provide just the right amount of light for an early evening with little ones. It is stronger than a nightlight, but enough to have a quiet, peaceful light. Putting one on top of an old fashioned doily on a bureau would be pleasant.

What we see around us in our homes affects our mood. When we decorate with gentle, pleasant things, we are calmer and more able to enjoy our babies and children. Harsh lights or gaudy colors can make us easily irritated and that would take away the happiness of a family. By taking the time to consider pleasant things to have around us, we can help create a peaceful, loving home.

As children get older, we can take their coloring pages and artwork and put them on the walls of the hallways. It is like their own little art gallery in a loving home. They will walk the halls and look at all the pretty things they made. Sometimes mothers like to draw and paint and can put their work up with the children. It shows that mother has an interest in the things the children like to do.

Perhaps some of the art contains words and verses, such as a Psalm or Proverb. These are extra special and would bring a solemn sense of happiness to a home. Children can certainly practice their letters by writing verses and illustrating them with flowers, birds, trees, or some nature scene to help make the paper more eye - catching and special. This type of art in the home is my favorite to see.

Baby gates are quite a necessity! If you have more than one floor of living space, you will need gates at the top and bottom of staircases. You may also want one at the kitchen door, or at the entrance of the living room. This is so that a toddler can play with the family without running off out of sight and into danger.

Porches also need a baby gate. Toddlers love to run outside on a large porch. If the gate is there, it will protect them from the dangerous steps. It will also make your time outdoors more peaceful, as the baby will know he is only allowed inside the gated area.

Every kitchen ought to have a high chair for baby. They make them so elaborate these days. I will always love the old wooden versions that my oldest was able to enjoy. It went beautifully with the rest of the dining room set. Now we have plastic chairs of all shapes and sizes. Some may like the more modern ones, but I like the plain ones.

A nice carriage can be kept in a closet. Many use these for taking walks or when they are on an outing. Carriages fit nicely in the trunk. I have folded mine up and even taken it on the bus! They are very handy. We usually kept our carriage open and ready for use throughout the house. Babies love taking walks indoors as well as outdoors.

Living rooms often contain a baby swing and playpen. As the family gathers around for the evening prayers, or Bible time, the baby is nearby. We used to have a large braided rug on our floor. It was humble and cozy. There was a large old lamp on an end table at each side of our couch. Father's recliner was just across from this. He had a table nearby and a TV stand as well. He could sit there and have coffee and cake in the late evening. The gentle light of the lamps helped make the memory of home a lasting, happy one.

II

The New Baby

It used to be that Daddy was not needed in the delivery room. He would pace the waiting room until he was called to see his new baby. Labor was more of a private matter for Mother. When it was all over, she would present the baby to her husband. They were both neat and fixed up from the ordeal. Today, fathers are almost required to be there for the birth. Many hospitals even provide an extra bed in the room for a husband to stay with his wife for the few days she is there. Twenty or thirty years ago, this just didn't happen. The husband would visit his wife during visiting hours. The rest of her stay was time for her to rest, and get used to taking care of the baby.

While in the hospital, the baby was always dressed in a white gown. Baby was gently wrapped in a receiving blanket. This was tucked under the arms on both sides so his little arms were free. It was so precious to be handed a snuggled up baby, a real bundle of joy!

Back at home, it was traditional for Mother to take complete charge of the infant. She dressed, fed, and changed the baby herself. Fathers worked to provide the living and left the majority of the care of the children to Mothers. Mom was already home as a devoted housewife. Home was her domain. She was the patient nurturer who was delighted to have a little baby to care for.

When Dad would come home from work, he would hold his dear baby for awhile. He might stand nearby and lend a hand when Mother did the bathing and dressing of baby. He would talk about his day at work and be grateful to be home with his little family, and enjoy the domestic scene.

A new mother would stay home to recover from the experience of birth. She protected the baby from germs by keeping him at home. A new baby was rarely seen in public. Home was the place for Mother and baby. This was where they were safe, and where they could enjoy the routine and quiet of home. Once the baby was established, after a few months, they might venture out to visit family or attend church. Today, it is common to see new mothers out in the stores with an infant not even a week old!

Visits to the home of a new mother were only done by close family members, such as the grandparents who were there to help. Friends and Neighbors would send a note, card, or food to show their help and care. They knew to give Mother some time to rest, and to get her home life established with the new little bundle.

Many babies cry almost constantly in the first several weeks. This is hard on everyone as they would worry and wonder how to ease and comfort the baby. Some fathers get grumpy or easily irritated, thinking there is some easy solution. This is the perfect time for Mom to snuggle up the baby and sit in the rocking chair. Sometimes quietly singing or humming a lullaby will help soothe the little one to sleep. At other times, pacing the floor may help as well. Just remember that as long as baby is changed, fed, and gently burped at regular times, (and not ill), there is little else to do but comfort and cuddle the child. This is a temporary phase and soon the baby will be more predictable and will cry less often.

It is tempting to hold a sweet baby all the time. But the child should be laid down in his crib for both awake time and while sleeping, as much as possible. The more he is used to being happily in the crib, the easier it will be for him to learn to fall asleep on his own. The crib will be familiar to him and he will be content. When baby is happy and content, he is able to fall asleep.

I used to keep notes as I fed my babies. Their own schedule would emerge as I would look over my notes from a few days. I knew how much they were happy eating, how often they wanted to eat, and when they were usually napping or sleeping at night.

Many years ago, a baby's schedule was almost a scientific theory. You were told how much to feed the baby and when to feed him. A baby's routine was created by Mother based on the doctor's advice. For instance, a new baby on formula would have 4 ounces every 4 hours. Or, something like 2 ounces every 2 hours.

Thirty years ago, formula was ready-made in large cans. Today, it is in powdered form and mothers are expected to mix it on their own. It is harder to know if one has measured it correctly, and feeding schedules are based on baby. Doctors today, when asked what to do, tell new mothers to feed a baby whenever they want, however much they want. This is confusing and causes inexperienced mothers to have babies with upset stomachs from overfeeding. A baby should not be drinking formula constantly. Formula takes longer to digest than nature's milk. A baby needs about an hour or two between feedings to rest and digest.

Babies who are nursed, on the other hand, can be nursed at any time. Generally speaking, if they have a complete feeding (a certain number of minutes on each side, with burping), they can wait an hour or two between feedings. If baby fell asleep during the feeding and mother had trouble waking him back up to finish, another feeding can happen right away. Babies digest nature's milk much faster than formula. Taking notes and keeping a diary of feeding times, and amounts, will help the mother see just what her baby needs.

A sponge bath for a new baby is all that is needed in the first several days. One can simply fill up a bowl, or basin, with warm water mixed with baby soap and put it on a little table nearby. A hooded towel and baby wash cloth are the bath time tools. Mother should put baby lotion on her hands and rub it together before putting it on the baby. This will take away the chill and warm it up. He also needs baby oil on the top of his head. Just apply with a little cotton ball, as if you are gently brushing the top of his hair. This should be applied daily to prevent cradle cap.

If there is a diaper rash, plain old Vaseline will protect the baby's skin while the rash is healing. To prevent a rash, powder should be applied at each diaper change.

In the first few weeks after birth, Mother needs help with housekeeping and meals. Mother needs her rest, but she also needs the household to continue to run smoothly. It is wonderful to have grandmother there during the confinement. It is also helpful to have the advice and experience of a trusted, veteran mother who will help ease any worries, and help with some of the baby care.

III

Stories, Playtime, and Rest

Children need an orderly home to keep them calm and secure. A regular routine is the way to make this happen. As baby grows up, napping, bedtime, and playtime tend to stay the same. The baby grows into a toddler and then into a small child, and his home routine ought to be fairly consistent. The child will know what to expect, and find happiness in the familiar activities of daily life.

In the morning, as the child wakes up, he might play for a little while, then have his breakfast. It used to be that the family would sit all together at the table. Dad and Mother would have their eggs and coffee. The children would have their oatmeal, toast, and milk. Baby would be in the highchair with pureed fruit and oatmeal. Today, it is not quite as common to have the family all together for meals. But if one can manage to do this, even in some small way, such as having Mother at the table with the children at least, it would bring a world of good to the family.

Unlike our modern American culture, television was never part of mealtime. The first TV- set was commonly placed in the living room. It had no part in the kitchen, interfering with the family's time of nourishment and fellowship.

Children learn their manners and are kept from being "wild" when they are not given the freedom to run around the house eating food anywhere they'd like. They most certainly should not be allowed to watch television or play games while they are eating. Having meals together is a time for visiting, and taking the time to eat the nourishment placed before all. If Mother is happily at the table, along with the children, she sets an example the children will follow.

Children must get "air," on a daily basis. This is the fresh air and sunshine they enjoy when outdoors. My grandmother used to advise that children needed at least one hour playing outside in order to have good health. This is harder, of course, in colder climates, particularly in the middle of a bitterly cold winter. In times of harsh weather, storms, and the like, children would need to remain indoors, doing something productive and active to keep them healthy.

When children have times of playing outside, once in the morning perhaps and then again in the afternoon, it helps them to get good and tired for naps and bedtime. It also brings a rosy color to their cheeks and helps keep them well.

There should be plenty of toys available for children to enjoy. These can be as simple as a set of plastic bowls and lids from the kitchen, or sets of blocks, dolls, cars, and trucks. These need not be expensive. Children have great imagination and will enjoy themselves with whatever toys you have on hand. As long as the house is pleasant and as calm as possible, without adults fighting or bringing in dramatic troubles, the children will be happily content at playtime. Here and there, it is good for Mother to sit in on their games and smile along with them before getting back to her housekeeping chores. The children will love it, and Mother will find joy in such activities with her little ones.

A house full of good books is a wise investment. These can be kept in bookcases, little crates, or even in a bucket. Small children would love to toddle over to the couch and find a basket of books nearby to browse through. Colorful board books are good for the youngest child. Easy readers and rhyming books are also highly enjoyable. Be careful in your choice of books in that they are instructive in Biblical ways, while entertaining and enjoyable to read.

There should be a story time each day. My favorite set of books to read to children is "Uncle Arthur's Bedtime Stories."

All my children have dearly loved these sweet, wholesome stories that teach faith in God, and kindness in the home.

In the afternoon, there should be a routine of sameness for naptime. Every day, the child should be hugged and held and slowly carried to his little bed. He should be kissed and told how nice that it was now naptime, or time for "night - night." His favorite blanket should be used and a happy routine of quietly settling him in for a time of sleeping should sweetly happen. Each family will have their own method for this, but if it is the same each day, at the same hour, it will become familiar and the child will go along without any trouble. Please be warned: if other members of the family are around or openly having fun "without him," he will not want to go to bed. The house should clear out, perhaps with whoever is at home going into other rooms and being quiet, while the child is being put down for a nap, then all should go well.

This should be the same type of routine for bedtime in the evening. Mother should decide at what hour the child must go to sleep. For some that may be 7 or 8 p.m. After supper-time and baths are finished, and perhaps some quiet, happy moments are spent with the family, it will be time to wind down the day. Evening and daytime should be very different so the child will sense that day is for being awake and night is for rest and sleep. The house may be louder and busier in the daytime, but evening is when the night has come, and with it - the quiet and slower pace. Dim lights in the house and little noise will help with the transition to bedtime. Sweet whispers and the quiet singing of hymns will help soothe the children to get ready for bed. Then as the child is hugged and kissed and prayed with, the child should be happily tucked into bed and snuggled with a favorite blanket. It is bedtime - a happy time to rest and sleep.

The night routine should be the same each night, week after week, month after month. If events call the family away for some fun, Mother should make every effort to get home in time for the supper, baths, and bedtime routine. This is a wonderful priority that the sameness of home can always be counted on. This helps children have security and a peacefulness about them.

IV

Nourishing Little Ones

It used to be that mostly wholesome, fresh foods were in the family kitchen. Processed and convenience foods did not enter the marketplace until sometime in the 1930's and 1940's. Families would have gardens to provide fresh fruits and vegetables all year round. Children knew where these delicious foods came from, and were often involved in part of the planting and harvesting of home gardens.

Family menus were also very basic. There was not a large variety of meals which were served. Today, consumers are encouraged to make all kinds of new foods to keep things "exciting." This is not a necessity. It is a luxury. Serving plain food that your own family liked was common and expected.

One of the biggest battles in our day is trying to keep our children away from sugary junk food. Friends and relatives want the children to have a "treat" and offer this type of food to them. Old time Mothers of today look overprotective and are considered to be "spoiling their fun" if we don't agree to the garbage they want to give our children. The way to counteract this is to make wholesome baked treats and snacks ourselves.

Homemade muffins can be made with applesauce instead of vegetable oil. We can add fresh, chopped apples and cinnamon. There are many excellent recipes in old cookbooks that will teach us how to make wholesome, fresh foods for our family. It is far superior to the processed, packaged, junk offered in the marketplace.

There are creative ways to add "boring" vegetables into dinner foods. Some examples: Lasagna can have a sauce made with blended fresh broccoli and grated carrots. Soups and stews can have a hint of fresh spinach, some celery, potatoes and carrots. Blueberries and strawberries can be added to milkshakes and put into muffins or pancakes. There are many ways to add good, wholesome food to the family menu.

If we study traditional cooking from the old cookbooks, we will keep our kitchen stocked with basics. This will make it easy to whip up banana bread, or make a hearty soup with homemade biscuits.

There will be little need to buy ready-made foods when we have artistic control of our stocked, homemade kitchens.

It used to be that everyone had to "clean their plate," by eating all that was served. It was considered rude and wasteful not to eat what was presented. In our homes today, we can consider the likes and dislikes of family members and be sensitive to this, by perhaps serving certain foods we know they would like. If your husband or child doesn't like asparagus, for example, try serving a fresh spinach salad with dressing. Once you know what each likes, these can be staple foods in your regular weekly diet.

One fun way for children to enjoy fresh vegetables is to have a time of "morning refreshments." This could be sometime between breakfast and lunch, after the children have been outside playing. Mother can place carrot sticks, broccoli, cheese, crackers and dipping sauce at the center of the table; or, perhaps a bowl of grapes and fresh blueberries. The children can all sit at the table with Mom and talk about how much fun they had outside. She can help herself to the snacks and tell the children to help themselves while they talk and visit.

I still serve this kind of treat when we have the grown children and grandchildren home for a visit. I ask if they are hungry and, even if they say "no," I place the refreshments on the table. I always see most everyone enjoying the food while we all talk.

"Tea time" is also a lovely old New England tradition. Some might have fresh coffee made in the afternoon, but I like to serve tea and hot chocolate. This is a wonderful time to sit at the table and play board games while enjoying a warm beverage with the family.

We must be careful, however, not to offer too many snacks or foods between meals. You've heard that old saying, "Don't spoil your dinner!" Children should be hungry and eager for their meals. This will give them a healthy appetite and make them appreciate the good cooking and good, nourishing food Mother has prepared.

The family table used to be the center of happy times and good food. In these modern days, it is the most forgotten piece of furniture in our homes. If we could just make the effort to enjoy our meals together at the old kitchen table, our families would benefit greatly.

V

Mother's Care

Under a Mother's guidance, love, and care a child is raised, trained, and taught to be a good citizen. At least that is what ought to happen. Sadly, modern children are encouraged to spend every day doing their own thing, and have an unhealthy focus on being entertained. This is the kind of culture we live in and it is hard not to be swept along with the latest theory, or "fad" in raising children.

We ought to take care of our babies and children. We need to see that they are nicely dressed. Mothers used to take pride in the way the little ones looked, even if the family was poor. A small child who looked dirty or unkempt was a mark on the mother. It meant that Mother was not doing her part.

Little ones need to dress warmly in the cooler months. Babies and small children need to wear hats to protect their ears and keep warm. They need to have well fitted coats. I love to see children in old fashioned wool, and homemade knits, rather than designer styles that only serve the purpose of showing off a fad.

Mother must be sure to keep the children clean and washed. Bathing and hair washing ought to be done on a daily basis. Throughout the day, they need to be cleaned up. If we are out on an errand, we can bring a package of baby wipes to wash little faces and hands while away from home. Children should be taken care of by being kept neat. A dirty, messy child, makes us think of a harried, haggard mother who is too overwhelmed to do her part in caring for her children. It should be a routine habit to work on keeping children clean.

We ought to teach our toddlers to help with the cleaning. We can teach them to help us wash highchair trays and help wash their little faces. I like to give them their own napkin at each meal. The kitchen table should have a napkin holder, and each one in the family ought to have a napkin beside their plate. Good manners means that we take that napkin and place it on our laps, and use as needed. Babies and small children see this example and learn their manners. They learn that staying neat and clean are good character qualities.

Children will certainly get messy when eating or when playing outdoors. We clean them when they are finished. It will be a nice habit they are used to. When they are older they will wash their own faces and hands and mother will monitor and praise the child for this.

Clean and neat clothes are also important. These need not cost a lot of money. Inexpensive clothing can be found very easily these days. There are different types of clothing - some for play, some for school, some for church, and some for outings. I never liked taking the children on errands in their play clothes. I would say, "We are going out, let's get washed up and dressed in something nice." We present the children to the public in pleasant clothes and this blesses those around us.

We must protect our little ones from harmful influences. We do this by being with them and teaching them rules of safety. We don't let them out of our sight in public. We ought to keep watch over what type of people come into our homes. We also protect our children from bad books and bad television programs. It seems that even cartoons are full of ungodliness these days. We guard their minds while they are too young to know what harm can come. Babies and children ought to be raised in sweet innocence as much as possible.

Modeling good manners is done by example. If mother says "please" and "thank you" to her children, they learn it as part of normal conversation. She ought to teach her children social skills and how to respond in different situations. For example, before meeting someone who is expected to visit, Mother will coach the child to say, "Nice to meet you," or "Hello." Just whatever their age allows them to say with good manners. Mother should teach kindness and hospitality each day to her children.

This all takes much work and effort and will most certainly be rewarded. The young years are the most crucial for training children and instilling good, virtuous character.

VI

Helping Create a Peaceful Home

When children are happy and pleasant, home is a lovely place to be. Mother can start training her children to be helpful in the early years. An important part of playtime is cleaning with Mother. This should happen at least twice each day – before lunch and before dinner preparation. Children as young as 2 years old can help clean up their toys and straighten up the house. When it is time for Mother to start cooking, she can settle the children down at the kitchen table with a fun project used only at this time of day – something as simple as coloring projects or play dough will keep children entertained long enough for Mother to make the evening meal.

I often give a dishcloth to a toddler to hand to the person about to wash dishes. The child smiles with pride as he gets to be helpful and glows with the accomplishment of a trusted responsibility.

When a new baby is brought into the house, the other children should be brought close to help with baby's care. We have all seen the Mother holding a precious baby but shooing away brother or sister and impatiently saying, "Not now! I am busy with the baby." This type of impatience shows a lack of love to the older children. It is dangerous. Mother has to take the extra time and care to include the other ones in the care of baby. She might say, "I will read you that book in just a minute. Will you help me snuggle up baby?" Or, perhaps she will say, "It is time to get the baby's bottle, come with me into the kitchen and we will do it together."

I still remember when my grandson was first introduced to his new baby sister. He didn't know what to think. Each day, whenever we heard her cry, I would look at him, eyes widened and say, "Oh no! Baby is crying!" We would both jump up together and run to her aid. We would soothe her, feed her, and talk to her. Each day, we taught him to care for and to love his sister in this way.

Babies get so much love and attention and this is important. The other children must get many hugs and kisses and affection just like before, if not more so. This will help make them sweet and tender towards the baby. They will want to watch out for her and protect her as she grows up, rather than resenting her for taking away Mother's love.

To avoid much misery and conflict in a home, I made sure children had assigned seating. This was for the kitchen table and also in our car. This saved a world of trouble and fighting over who would sit where. From the very beginning, each had their own seat and that never changed. There was also a privilege for the oldest who was assigned the front seat. If at any time the oldest was not present, the next oldest got the front. But the backseat assignments never changed. The children were used to this and never fought about it. It is the same with the kitchen table seats. Each knew their place. Each knew they had their very own spot and were happy.

This can also happen with cups, towels, and toothbrushes. Each child had their own color to avoid conflict and fighting. One might have the color blue. This meant that blue was "Elizabeth's" and she always had the blue toothbrush, blue towel, and blue cup. No one used her things because each had his own color and was secure and happy with it. This may seem like such a little thing, but it will save many years of yelling, arguing, and crying about fairness and whose turn it may have been to have a certain cup or which color toothbrush someone wanted. It really made life more pleasant to have assigned colors.

I like to have the children make or buy inexpensive gifts for each other on birthdays and holidays. They get so excited to think about each other and want to make the other one happy. This helps build their love and family bonds.

Practicing hospitality in the home is another way to have peaceful children who generally get along. One might make a special snack to surprise a sister or brother. This is common kindness which delights the heart. I loved to help and guide the children in these endeavors. They would also watch me do the same for their father. Did he want some dessert and coffee? Well, one of the children would help me serve it to him. He would always be grateful and happy to receive such a gift.

When a small child is ill and resting, the siblings can be called in to help amuse and entertain the little one. They can also help by getting a cold washcloth, fresh sheets, cold drinks and other such home hospital needs. This teaches them to have servant's hearts and to care for one another.

Teaching children how to live peacefully together takes patience and creativity. These sweet skills they learn in the home form their character and help make them kind as they grow into adulthood.

VII

Gentle Care of Finances

These days, many people spend large sums of money on entertainment, leisure activities, and an excess of food. This is the way our culture is set up in these modern days. This is not the traditional way for a family. Husbands and wives would dream about having babies and looked forward to their arrival. When the children started to arrive into a sweet home, Mom and Dad were congratulated and looked at with a sweet sense of respect. They were a settled family and were blessed with children.

The money needed to feed, clothe, and house children was provided by Dad's labor, and Mother's careful use of the household money.

Wholesome food was made from scratch. It is cheaper and more nutritious this way. Basic foods were served and enjoyed at the family table.

Baby clothes were often given to a new mother, which she carefully laundered and took care of for future babies. To buy a basic layette set for baby doesn't cost nearly as much as people may think. One will need a certain amount of gowns, sleepers, undershirts ("onesies"), little socks, a coat and hat, and receiving blankets.

When a new baby was expected, nobody knew if it was going to be a boy or a girl. An ultrasound procedure was not commonly done until the 1990's. Before that, you didn't know what your baby was until birth. Because of this, layette sets were sold in neutral colors - like pale peach, white, soft yellows, and pastel greens. These were wonderful because you would use the same layette set for all your babies. Both boys and girls wore the same things until they were a bit older. Then dresses were made or bought for a little girl, and little shirts and overalls, or pants, were obtained for the boys. The clothes were cared for, and mended, by mother so they could be re-used for each child. Only on a rare occasion was a special outfit bought for a child. This was then saved for the younger siblings. In this way, clothing needs were limited and not a drain on the household budget.

It was unheard of for children to require separate bedrooms. It was common for several children to be together in one room, or 2 rooms - one for the boys, and one for the girls. The children were used to this and often enjoyed the company and companionship of one another. Here is where they learned to share space and to get along with others. Here is where they learned to keep things neat so as not to annoy each other.

Bunk beds are a wonderful invention. Many rooms can have one or two sets, easily sleeping 2 to 4 children to a room. The children love this and it helps keep the rooms neat. Many children used to share closets and bureaus, taking 2 drawers each, or 1/3 of the closet. There was no need, or room, for an excess of clothing or an abundance of personal belongings.

There is no need for large, elaborate housing. This would be a luxury and limited to the rich. Simple living is what keeps costs down. A small home - such as 3 bedrooms with 1 bath - was normal.

I realize we are told that we need a guest bath, and 2 to 3 bathrooms are considered a modern necessity. It is almost funny how our nation went from having an outhouse at the back of the house, to requiring several indoor baths! Most of today's grandmothers grew up in a home with only one bathroom. We would use a schedule. For example, we would find out what time someone had to be at work or school, and set times for shower usage. We didn't blink an eye if we had to get up an hour or two earlier just to have plenty of time to take a turn in the shower. Each person had their own 20 to 30 minutes and didn't have to share the room. There were even reputable boarding houses where the floor (of perhaps 6 guests) had one common bath. People certainly did not take too long on personal grooming, and they didn't waste water. That would have been unfair to the other tenants.

The cost of caring for a baby is very minimal if the Mother nurses the child and uses cloth diapers. There is a lot of work, but not much money is needed. I remember when I had two little girls (19 months and 3 months), both in cloth diapers. At the time I could afford to buy disposable diapers but wanted to save some money for other things. I had no dryer but lived in a cute little house near Cape Cod. There was a small laundry room near my kitchen. I would keep a bucket for the used diapers near the washer. After I did the daily wash, I placed the diapers on a wooden drying rack next to a heater in the cozy kitchen. Make sure you use special detergent and fabric softener to keep the diapers soft. You will also need a set of "rubber pants," to go over the diapers. Those little diaper pins are also very cute and it is almost nostalgic to use them.

Years later, I tried using cloth diapers with my last baby. At that time I was so busy and tired that I felt it was more important to spend the money on disposable diapers.

As children grow up, they help more and more around the house. They are not a drain on the family but a wonderful asset. Their work and help with frugality builds character, but also helps build the family legacy.

When children are grown, they are able to work and earn their own living. They also want to help their elderly parents because they grew up in a loving, hard working home. It is a wonderful blessing to have a large family to enjoy in old age.

VIII

A Sweet Disposition

One of the goals of motherhood is to be calm and sweet. When I was growing up, it was a lot easier. Around 4 p.m. in the evening, in my neighborhood, as you walked down the street, each home had a mother preparing supper for her family. All the mothers were home and there were wonderful smells of home cooking.

There was a quiet routine in the afternoons as the day wound down. Nobody was rushing off for games or appointments. No one had ambitious ideas about competitions or events for their children. Everyone went home for family time and to eat together. Home was the priority. Then children would do their homework, perhaps play outside for a little while, and then come in for bedtime.

Dad was the one with all the worries and stress from the working world. When he came home each night, it was like stepping into another world. Home was the calm respite from the world. It was a happy place. Mom was glad to see him and greeted him with a genuine smile. My husband says that a Mother is "sheltered." She is safe at home and protected from the realities of the harsh world. This helps keep her sweet.

In those early years, there was no such thing as Cable Television or news broadcasted 24 hours a day. The news came on at 6 in the evening, or you could read about it in the daily paper. We were not kept in high anxiety with a constant flow of horror stories brought into our homes. Those were more idealistic days. Today, many can choose not to have cable or not to have a television. They can choose not to check the news on computers at all hours of the day and night. This is a personal decision. For me, I hear whatever news comes in from my husband or grown children, here and there. But mostly, I am protected and gratefully "sheltered" from the world. I am able to have a sweet spirit and a slow-paced, kind demeanor because I am not stressed from every angle.

Dressing nicely and modestly has a gentling effect on a Mother. Clothing styles of today are hard to take. Most of what is offered is uncomfortably tight and strangely arranged.

Mothers no longer dress like Mothers. They are often given choices of teen clothing in larger sizes. I love the old styles of a regular dress with a cardigan sweater over it. Add a necklace, pretty pair of shoes, a nice hairstyle, and Mom will both feel and look lovely. She will look motherly and sweet. Presenting oneself in a pleasant way brings forth kind manners, and also respectful consideration.

Patience with husband and children will help avoid a world of stress. Developing a forgiving nature is also essential. These traits are a constant exercise in selflessness. We, like our husbands and children, are frail and will make mistakes. I remember once, years ago, I had carefully made a plate of food for someone's lunch. Somehow it slipped out of my hand and onto the floor, right in front of one of my teenagers who it belonged to. The look on that child's face was priceless. I was so sorry, but my child understood and helped me clean up the mess. Many times this same child had accidentally spilled milk and made messes of his own. All the children have from time to time. We just smile and do our best to work together to clean it up. This is part of a forgiving nature and one that understands we have to be patient with each other's mistakes.

I remember one year, one of the children accidentally knocked a bowl of leftover sauce out of the refrigerator. There was a sad mess all over the place, splattered everywhere! I would not have dreamed of asking that child to clean it up. It was too much for the inexperienced to bear. So I helped and while I helped, the child learned that one little step at a time, with someone to help, got the work done and made the task almost pleasant. We laughed and talked while we worked, and this kept our spirits uplifted.

A slow - paced Mother who is not overburdened with outside cares has the best chance of a gentle, kind-hearted outlook. When she is gentle and sweet, this helps the children to love her, and to love home.

IX

To Love is To Sacrifice

I realize it is very hard work to be a mother. Just thinking about all she has to do in the home is exhausting. Her work is one of sacrifice. She gives up the prime of her life to the raising of a family. This is why mother should be synonymous with the word virtuous.

Part of lovingly raising children requires discipline. We need to teach and train our children. The best training ought to happen in the early years. This makes the road to growing up much easier for the family.

A child cannot be left to himself. He needs guidance and wise direction. His job is certainly to play and be happy, but also to learn to follow rules and instruction. Children will not always want to do what Mother says. This will cause conflict at times. Yet this is necessary for the good of the child.

Here are some ideas that may help:

1. <u>Don't offer choices to young ones</u>. For example, I would not say, "Would you like macaroni and cheese or peanut butter and jelly for lunch?" You, as the Mother, must serve what you feel is best. The child has no reason to complain unless he is offered a choice and then can't make up his mind. It is an unnecessary problem that can be avoided. Another example is the modern idea of allowing little ones to choose their own clothes. Mother chooses the clothes and the child wears them. End of story. (gentle smiles). There is no sense in prolonging the day waiting for a small child to take on worries he certainly doesn't need. His mind is too young and immature, and this idea of "choices" is not good for his character. Allowing a child to choose for himself is a privilege that must be earned. It is also a responsibility that comes with age and maturity.

2. <u>Teach children how to behave in public</u>. I would not take tired, hungry children out on errands unless there was an emergency. They would only act up because they would be over - stimulated and off their routine. Outings should happen around the child's normal schedule - after breakfast is often a good time, doing one's best to make sure the family is back home in time for lunch and a nap. When the outing happens on schedule, talk about what you are going to do in the store,

how long you will be, and what is expected. Will you buy the child a drink or snack? Don't allow a child to "pick out what he wants" in the store. Make it clear in advance exactly what you will buy him. When children know what is happening, and the routine is the same, they will tolerate the errands more pleasantly.

Babies and small children belong in a shopping carriage. I would not let them walk around. The store is not a playground. It is too stimulating and overwhelming for a small child to be allowed to walk around at the market or shopping center. Walking beside mother, holding the carriage, is a privilege earned when he is older.

3. <u>Don't let a small child win an important battle</u>. For example: I have a beautiful set of toddler - size rocking chairs. These were given to me 23 years ago. All of my five children have enjoyed using them. They are still in like - new condition. Now my grandchildren are using them. I put them in our nursery for my grandson to use. One day, I noticed he was playing with one of them, tipping it upside down. This was not allowed. He has other chairs, plastic, which I don't mind him playing with, but the rocking chairs had to be taken care of. I was stern with him, saying, "We don't do that." I was willing to remove the chairs from the room, later when he wasn't looking (we handle one battle at a time), until he was a little older and more responsible. But because of the tone of my voice, and my firmness, he stopped the behavior. He knows that

grandmother is sweet and gentle with him, loves to read him stories, and give him lots of hugs. He knows that a stern voice is a rare thing and only used in important cases, so he listened.

In another case, sometimes a child will be overtired and not want a bath. He may yell and squirm and try to avoid the bath. In our house, no matter how tired any of us are, the bath happens every evening at the same time. It is non-negotiable. A Mother may be willing, without anger, to do her best to give the bath despite the crying child. Sometimes, once a toddler is actually in the tub and Mother offers to read a book, in a kind soothing voice, the child will settle down enough to have the bath go well. Having a few toys in the tub helps make bath time pleasant for children. Little ducks and boats are always enjoyable.

4. <u>Tune out the crying when necessary</u>. If a child is attempting to throw a tantrum, remain calm and go about your normal routine. A child will learn that selfishness and greedy demands do not win him what he wants. Give in to the tantrum and you have rewarded and taught selfishness and bratty behavior. Not all children throw fits. Many who do have a strong will and may have fits many times. A Mother needs great patience to wait out these lessons her little one is learning.

5. <u>Punish for wrongdoing, but not for every fault</u>. There is a difference between right and wrong. Please don't confuse opinions, preferences, or annoying antics for wrong behavior.

6. <u>To avoid lying in small children, never ask why they did something</u>. They will think of all kinds of stories to get out of trouble. We want our children to be honest and trustworthy. By asking them why they did something wrong, you are creating a pattern where they will learn to lie to you on a regular basis. Instead, deal with the fault, forgive, and move on. Children, like we adults, have a sin nature. It should be no surprise that they will do things wrong. The goal is to train them through these mishaps and guide them to a noble life.

While discipline is often an unpleasant part of life, children are a wonderful joy and a blessing. Troublemaking by little ones is not something that happens often in a happy, orderly home. On those hard days, we might fall into bed praying for strength. We might also thank God that "Today, we made it through the day!" We should be proud of patiently enduring those lessons that were necessary, while not being lazy in our mothering.

Most of our time with them should be playing, enjoying fresh air, watching their faces light up when they see something exciting in nature, and teaching them beautiful songs and stories. Meal time, play time, and bedtime are all lovely experiences with our babies. There is great joy in being a Mother.

X

A Godly Heritage

Many years ago I bought several copies of an old hymn book. There was one for each of my five children. It didn't matter if they were old enough to read yet, they were to have a copy. From the time they were very young, we would read through the songs at our leisure. We also sang many of the songs each day, during our Bible time. Now grown, the children are familiar with "Rock of Ages;" "Amazing Grace;"and "Bringing in the Sheaves." These are etched in their memories from their childhood home, when they sang with Mother.

No matter what our children do in their adult years, whether they walk that godly path, or stumble along the way, there should have been laid a strong foundation of faith in God and the blessing of a solid Biblical education. The time to teach this to our children is when they are little. We teach best when we love the lesson ourselves.

I once read about Jewish children who were taken into convents and little Catholic schools to save their lives, when the Holocaust was going on overseas. Mothers and Fathers wept secretly, so as not to alarm the little ones, as they brought their beloved children to the nuns for safekeeping. There was a mighty fear and parents were being killed. The children were fed and clothed and kept safe in the nun's schools. They stayed there for years during the war and learned all about the Catholic religion and regular schooling as well. When the war was over, a Rabbi came to the school to gather up the Jewish children. He was told that it was impossible to know which ones were Jewish as they all had been taught alike. The Catholic children were mixed with the Jewish children. But the Rabbi knew something very special. He knew that every single little boy and girl was taught a special prayer at bedtime by their Mothers. He knew that if he waited for the children to go to bed, he could tell which ones were Jewish. The children said their prayers and got into their beds while the Rabbi waited by the door. When they were settled, he called out in a loving, clear voice:

"Shema Yisrael.

Hear, O Israel, the Lord our God, the Lord is One."

[From Deut. 6:4 - 9]

A Crying of homesickness was heard throughout by the Jewish children, as they remembered their sweet Mothers and that familiar prayer which was taught to them years ago. This was how the Rabbi knew which children were the Jewish ones. He was able to reclaim them and take them back to Jewish homes.

A Mother has the greatest influence over her children. She has the main job of teaching her children about the Lord and teaching them how to live a holy life. Her example and love for godliness is what will endear the children to the old paths and have a heart for God.

A daily time of Bible reading is one of the most important things she can do with the children. She should read, or have the children read to her, a passage here and there, or a chapter or two as the children's ages allow. This will help them have the desire to sit quietly and listen. Children will learn reverence and respect when it is approached with a quiet, devoted expectation of something wonderful, as they get to hear the word of God.

Mother should pray at each mealtime with the children. She should teach them prayers, praying with them at bedtime, and whenever a need arises. This should be a familiar pattern of daily living in a godly home.

Singing hymns with the children and teaching them sweet songs will stay in their hearts and teach them the godly path.

Try to find a good Church and take the children there. This precious weekly habit is becoming almost non-existent in these modern days. Good churches are hard to find. Once you find one, teach the children the delight in getting all dressed up and going to worship. Hearing a sermon each week is wonderful nourishment for the soul.

There is great honor in being the Mother who gets to teach and guide the children on that Heavenly path home. One day there will be tears of gratitude and joy as the children follow their Mother's heart Heavenward.

Appendix

"The Light in a Messy House"

(An article by Mrs. White to encourage the old fashioned Mother.)

Coffee is spilled on the counter and lower cabinets. Towels are on the floor. Personal belongings are all over the dining room chairs. Scattered toys create a walking hazard. Through this daily mess Mother walks about putting it all to rights. She wipes up the spills as they happen. She clears the crumbs, neatens the toys, and directs helpers to tidy the rooms. She is the light of cheerfulness who creates happiness and order in a messy home. She is the skilled laborer working in God's fields.

I have been told there are thousand year old vineyards which have been taken care of throughout the generations by skilled workers who are diligent. A preacher once visited one and noticed there was a forest all around the property, but the vineyard was well kept and noticeably different. He said you could see, from a great distance, that the vineyard was separate from the woods. There was a distinct line. You saw beauty in the well kept ground, and you saw wildness in the untamed forest.

This vineyard can also be like our homes. We are the diligent gardeners who clear the weeds, prune the vines, gather the fruit, and keep up that distinct line that separates our homes from the world.

The weeds and the vines and the pruning are all the things we do when we clean and bake and care for the family. Each day we do this with great skill and love. It eventually becomes a natural habit to the point that we often don't notice all the things we are doing in a day. We bring order and loveliness to our home vineyards. We bring the light of godliness and holiness to our little cottages.

Each time we clean a messy house, each moment we pick up and tend the home, it is a reminder of the world and all the damage sin is constantly causing. We are the salt of the earth. We are the light of the world. If the salt and the light are taken out of the home, we will see a piling up mess, which shows neglect. That distinction of the old vineyard and the forest will become marred and tangled up together to the point that the forest will take over the vineyard. We will not let that happen to our homes.

We housewives are the light of our homes. We spread happiness and sunshine through our cheerfulness and willing work. It is just like we are the lights in this dark, corrupt world. The next time you feel like you are cleaning the same messes over and over again, doing the same things over and over again, day after day; month after month; year after year; generation after generation, just remember that it is similar to how we, as God's people, shine a light of holiness amidst the constant mess of a sinful world. You are like the *vineyard keeper* and are desperately needed to keep that distinction clear.

Books by Mrs. White

Mother's Faith

For the Love of Christian Homemaking

Early Morning Revival Challenge

Mother's Book of Home Economics

Living on His Income

Old Fashioned Motherhood

About the Author

Mrs. White is a housewife of more than a quarter of a century, a beloved mother of five children, and grandmother of four. She is the granddaughter of revival preacher, LD Murphy. She lives in an 1800's house in rural Vermont.

For more information or to find Mrs. White's books, please visit:

The Legacy of Home Press

http://thelegacyofhomepress.blogspot.com

Also see Mrs. White's blog:

http://thelegacyofhome.blogspot.com

"That was when mothers rocked cradles and didn't leave the baby in the nursery while she worked in the factory or didn't hire baby sitters while she went to the movies or club.

Then mothers nursed their babies and loved them. Mother's arms were the safest haven, the surest comfort, until they learned to trust the Saviour."

 - Evangelist, Dr. John R. Rice (1895 – 1980), from his sermon, "Thank God for Good Mothers!"

Made in the USA
Coppell, TX
07 May 2022

77526852R10037